ELF OWL
· AND HIS ECOSYSTEM ·

Written by Megan Noel
Cover design by Robin Fight
Illustrated by Tanya Glebova

A glorious rainbow of brilliant colors streaks the sky as the burning sun begins to sink behind the hot, sandy dunes of the Sonoran Desert. Suddenly, as the first stars begin to twinkle overhead, a rather high-pitched chuckling sound breaks the evening stillness. It continues on and on, as if something is very funny. Who could that be?

1

The curious noises can be traced beyond a riot of colorful wildflowers to a nearby forest of towering saguaro cacti, which are not found naturally anywhere else in the world. A closer look reveals that this "laughter" doesn't belong to a person at all. This is the call of the smallest of all owls—the elf owl! Can you spot him?

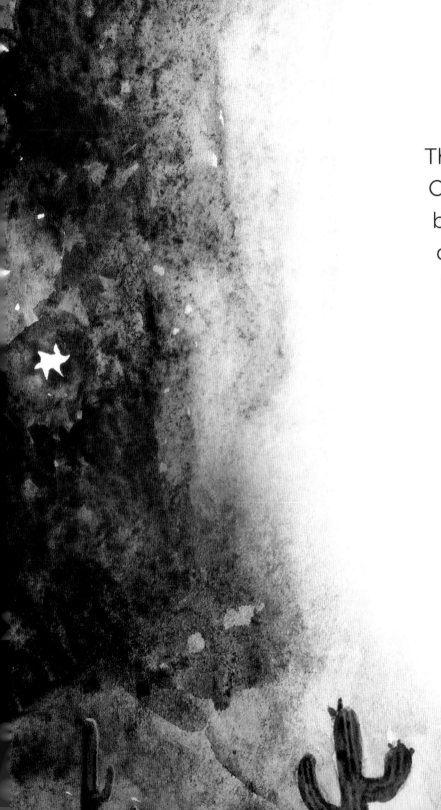

There he is! It is springtime, and Elf
Owl has just recently returned to his
breeding grounds here in the arid
desert ecosystem of southern Arizona.
Elf owls never build their own nesting
sites, so he has chosen to move into
an abandoned Gila woodpecker
hole, high in this sturdy saguaro.
Now he must defend his territory
and attract a mate with which to
share his new home, so he calls out
across the moonlit landscape.

Because the bright desert days are hot, many other creatures are also just beginning to stir as the daylight fades away. Crickets, katydids, and other nocturnal insects raise their chirping chorus. They sustain elf owls and many other creatures in this hot, dry climate with their protein and water content.

An antelope jackrabbit emerges from his shady daytime hideout beneath a palo verde tree, bounding across the sand in search of a prickly pear cactus to nibble on. His enormous ears are ever on the alert for dangerous predators. In the distance, a coyote's eerie moan echoes off the walls of a canyon and is answered with barks and wails from his pack.

Darkness has almost settled in, but Elf's large, round, yellow eyes have no trouble spotting the flutter of a moth's wings as it flits around a clump of brittlebushes, busily pollinating the yellow blooms. Elf patiently waits for the ideal opportunity before swooping down to claim his dinner.

Although moths have the greatest sense of hearing in the animal kingdom, this moth didn't hear her tiny predator approach. Elf's silent flight is due to the clever design of his wings. The edges are equipped with soft white feathers that mute his wingbeats. After eating his fill of moths, the satisfied owl returns home.

In the middle of the night,
a bobcat prowls among the
saguaros. Elf knows that bobcats
are skilled climbers, so he takes
advantage of the camouflage his
grayish brown feathers provide and
remains quiet and still.

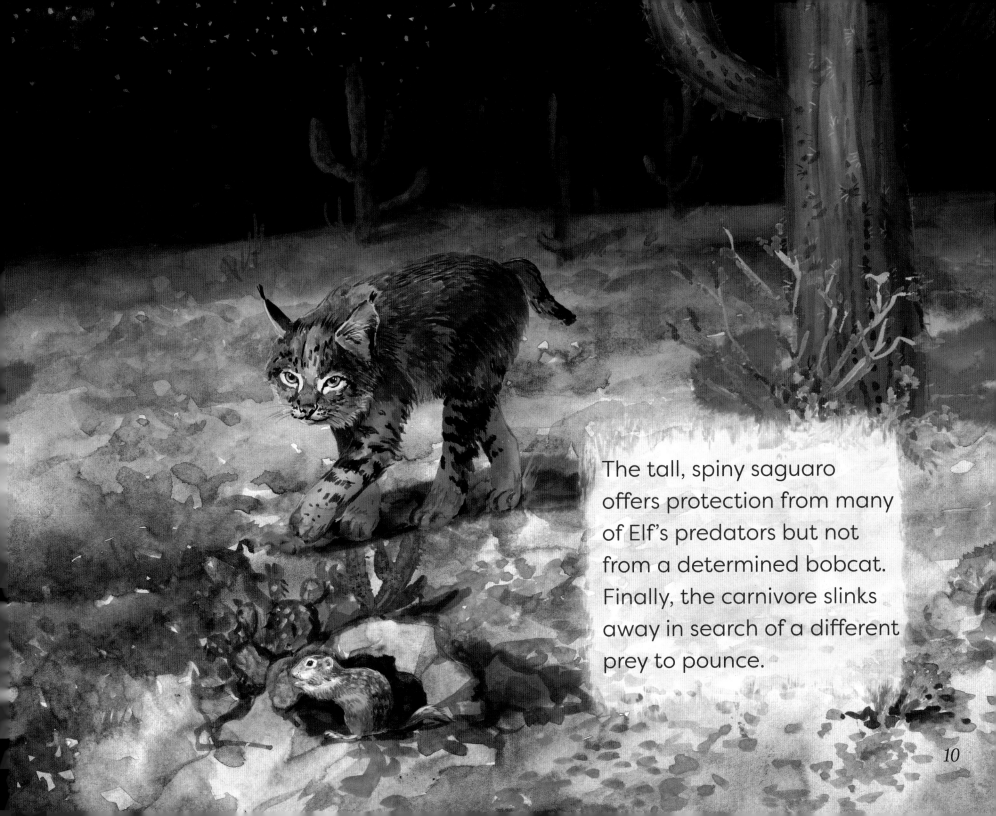

The tall, spiny saguaro offers protection from many of Elf's predators but not from a determined bobcat. Finally, the carnivore slinks away in search of a different prey to pounce.

As the darkness gives way to the day, Elf prepares to weather another stifling hot day by snuggling down into the cool shadows of his saguaro and tucking his weary head beneath his wing.

But while Elf Owl and many other desert creatures sleep the day away, life continues all around their shady dens. The Sonoran Desert is so wondrously diverse that many different species can be spotted going about their daily lives at any time of day or night.

A javelina ambles down the path of a winding arroyo, a dry streambed that will undergo a drastic change when the powerful summer monsoon storms begin. He is searching for a good resting spot in the shade to escape the intense midday sun.

Overhead, a small group of four hungry Harris's hawks soar gracefully, teaming up to chase a diamondback rattlesnake out of its hiding place in the desert scrub.

A pink-and-black-banded Gila monster creeps out of the cool comfort of his burrow, concealed beneath a small rocky outcrop. He spends most of the day in his underground lair and doesn't like to waste much time and energy on hunting. Easy prey such as eggs and unattended young make up most of his diet.

Heavy gray clouds are rolling into the desert on a southern wind, carrying moisture from the Pacific Ocean and Gulf of California and providing some relief from the blazing sun. The summer monsoon season has arrived, one of two rainy seasons that make the Sonoran Desert the wettest and most biodiverse desert in the world.

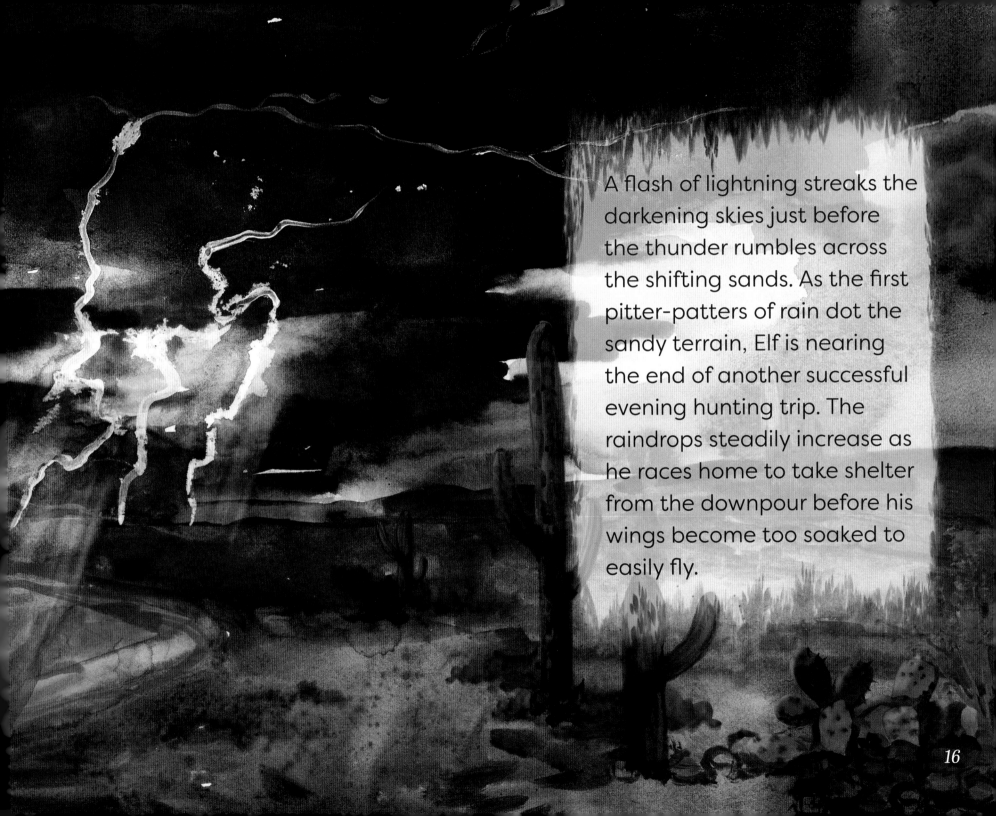

A flash of lightning streaks the darkening skies just before the thunder rumbles across the shifting sands. As the first pitter-patters of rain dot the sandy terrain, Elf is nearing the end of another successful evening hunting trip. The raindrops steadily increase as he races home to take shelter from the downpour before his wings become too soaked to easily fly.

The desert is refreshed by the arrival of the monsoon season with its brief storms. Here and there a creosote bush adds a splash of cheerful yellow, or the tall, spiky stems of an ocotillo wave in the wind with sprays of red spouting from their tops like flames. Pretty purple petals adorn the mighty ironwood trees.

Animals become more active, too, as they relish the chance to lap up the fresh water from the arroyo, which has been transformed into a running stream. Many find mates, including a desert tortoise who wades across the arroyo to nod at a female and bump noses in greeting.

18

There is a sweet fragrance in the air this evening as the moon casts its pale glow upon the clusters of delicate white blossoms that are open at the tips of many of the saguaros. Elf Owl has barely begun his nightly chatter when he hears an answering yip-yip-yip from a female perched on a palo verde.

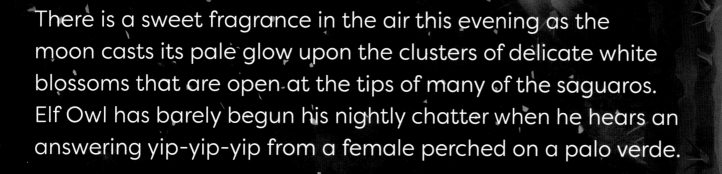

As she watches, he dive-bombs a centipede skittering down the tree, unbothered by its stings. He then presents it to the impressed female. Elf Owl has found his mate at last! Perhaps they will be a pair for life, which is common for many owl species.

Lesser long-nosed bats pick up the tantalizing
scent of the saguaro blooms, too, as their colony
leaves its nearby cave roost for the night. These bats survive
solely on the nectar from cactus flowers, making them the
Sonoran Desert's best nighttime pollinators. The life-giving
pollen dusts their furry heads as they drink their fill of the
sweet nectar, and they spread the yellow
powder to each lovely flower. They
play a vital role in holding this fragile
ecosystem together.

Since the blooms only last through one night and day, many birds and insects follow the pleasant melon-like aroma to the short-lived treat. A white-winged dove floats in for one last drink of the sticky nectar before returning to her hidden nest tucked safely in the middle of a cholla cactus, protected by its rough spikes.

Soon Elf's mate has begun to incubate three small, speckled eggs, and it is his duty to provide food for them both.

One evening, about three weeks later, Elf finds the first of three little owlets breaking free of her shell. Her brother and sister are not far behind, and the tiny, sparsely feathered newborns waste no time in letting their parents know they are hungry. Elf flies out alone in search of food for his family, but Mother will join him in a couple weeks.

As Elf prepares to strike at a juicy katydid, he is unaware that another pair of yellow eyes is watching him from its perch in an abandoned hawk's nest, hidden within the foliage of an ancient ironwood tree. The elf owl is not the only desert-dwelling owl that is gifted with silent flight, so Elf is taken by surprise when a great horned owl suddenly captures him midair in her strong, sharp talons!

Elf is not an aggressive bird by nature, and he knows that his small stature is no match for the much larger predator. As the great horned owl approaches her ironwood tree, Elf quickly employs his trickiest defensive tactic—playing dead. The young great horned owl relaxes her tight grip on his limp body, no longer concerned that her prey may try to escape.

But our little friend does escape! As soon as Elf darts free, he spots a hollow in the sturdy old ironwood with an opening just big enough for him to squeeze into.

When his instincts tell him the danger has passed, he snags a few beetles from his hideaway and zooms back across the arroyo to the safety of his own home.

Though the rain has stopped for now, a thick blanket of clouds still blots out the night sky. Neither moon nor stars can be seen tonight as Elf soars out to hunt. Although he can see very well in dim light, his night vision isn't as keen as many other owl species. Instead, he relies on his excellent hearing on these pitch-black nights.

Gliding out over the arroyo near his home, Elf hears a few desert toads splashing around in the shallow waters, but he ignores them when he hears a rustling below.

As the raging storms begin to dwindle, the water trickling through the arroyos evaporates into the hot, dry atmosphere. Toads hop away from the disappearing puddles to bury themselves in the sand, where they will patiently wait for the arroyos to be brought back to life by next summer's monsoons. The desert returns to its usual parched state, and many plants go dormant as they wait for the winter rain.

He quickly scoops up a scorpion with his tiny sharp claws and returns home, where he will carefully remove its stinger before giving it to his eager offspring.

28

By this time the trio of owlets are testing their wings, but Mom and Dad are still helping them find food. They will stay close by, keeping their watchful eyes on their young for at least a week after they fledge.

For the past several nights, Elf Owl has noticed a chill in the dry September air as he pokes his head out of the saguaro he has called home for the past six months. His little ones have now left the nest, and each night he finds fewer insects to feast upon. They are burrowing deep underground and will not resurface until the following spring.

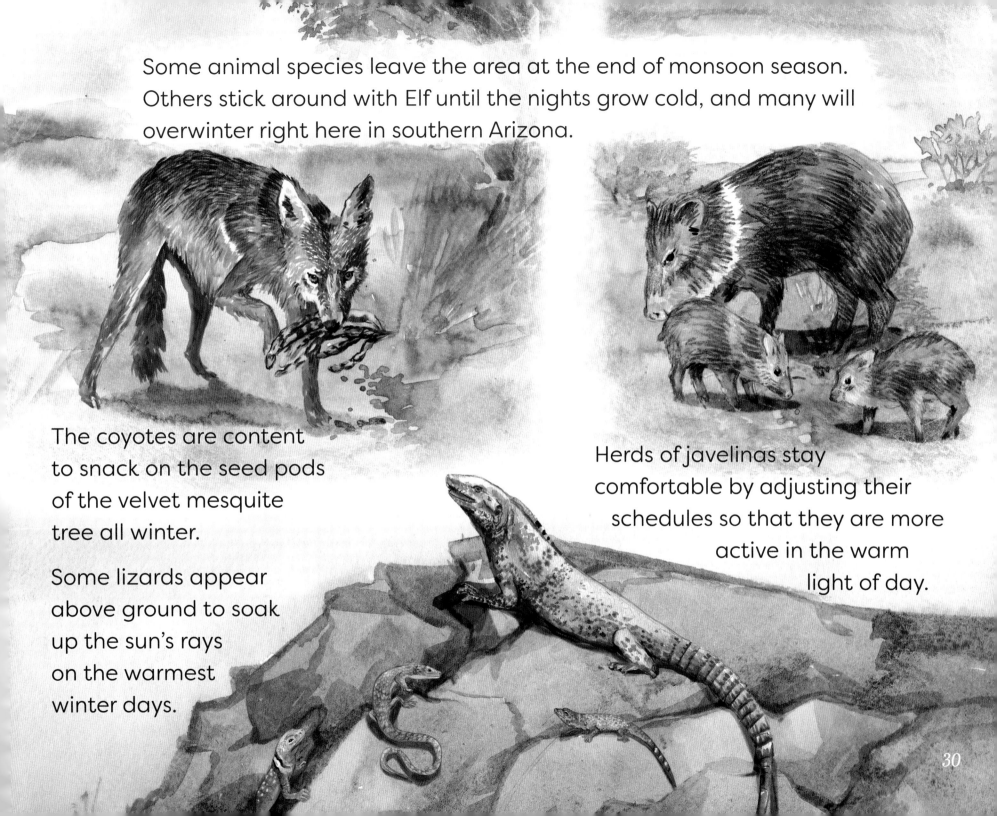

Some animal species leave the area at the end of monsoon season. Others stick around with Elf until the nights grow cold, and many will overwinter right here in southern Arizona.

The coyotes are content to snack on the seed pods of the velvet mesquite tree all winter.

Some lizards appear above ground to soak up the sun's rays on the warmest winter days.

Herds of javelinas stay comfortable by adjusting their schedules so that they are more active in the warm light of day.

But for Elf Owl, the time has come to move along. He will travel south to Mexico to spend the next six months where the nights are always warm and the insects always plentiful. Elf spreads his wings and takes flight, sure to return to the Sonoran Desert's uniquely diverse ecosystem when spring comes again.

31

Printed in China